ENTREPRENEURSHIP FOR THE YOUNG CEO

J. Domino Financial Group

In this workbook:

We introduce the young mind to entrepreneurship by finding out what moves them.

Higher education beyond high school is touched upon by way of not just college. Other forms of education - trade schools, certificates, jobs and careers are talked about as well as alternatives that can satisfy educational requirements towards a rewarding future.

Credit, debit, assets, and liabilities are introduced to help with a better understanding of what money is and isn't.

As a bonus, we discuss "Black Wall Street".

Defining: "Entrepreneurship"

Lastly, a small business plan is worked on as a beginning blue print to start our very first business venture.

The J. Domino
FINANCIAL GROUP
Partners in Money Management

Copyright © 2016 by Jewel L. Domino Group LLC

All rights reserved. No part of this publication may be reproduced, distributed, or transmitted in any form or by any means, including photocopying, recording, or other electronic or mechanical methods, without the prior written permission of the publisher, except in the case of brief quotations embodied in critical reviews and certain other noncommercial uses permitted by copyright law.

For permission requests, write to the publisher, addressed "Attention: Permissions Coordinator," at the address below.
Jewel L. Domino Group LLC
5 Lawrence Street, Unit 328
Bloomfield, NJ 07003
jeweldominof@gmail.com
www.vondorinstitute.org

Ordering Information:
Quantity sales. Special discounts are available on quantity purchases by corporations, associations, and others. For details, contact the publisher at the address above.
Orders by U.S. trade bookstores and wholesalers. Please contact for big distribution: Tel: (201) 259-6446; Fax: (908) 258-7959 or visit www.vondorinstitute.org or email:
info@vondorinstitute.org
Printed in the United States of America
Publisher's Cataloging-in-Publication data
Introduction to Entrepreneurship for the Young CEO
Title of book: a subtitle of the same book / Entrepreneurship for the Young CEO; Author: Jewel L. Domino.
1. The main category of the book – Entrepreneurship
ISBN-13: 978-0692694640 (Jewel L. Domino)
ISBN-10: 0692694641

First Edition

The J. Domino
FINANCIAL GROUP
Partners in Money Management

THANK YOU FOR BELIEVING IN ME

"family is air, family is water, family is food, family is love!"
Jewel L. Domino

To my parents, *Mr. & Mrs. Lonny A. Domino* - you are my king and queen

To my little girl, *Belle* – you are my little big girl trooper for going to work with me and being a professional when I had meetings. I love my princess.

To my brother, *Saladin* – thanks for keeping Belle happy when I'm away and thanks for the *money*. ☺

To my son, *John* – thanks for the idea of the program. You are so intelligent but just too damn lazy! I love you still.

Last but not least, to my ex-husband – Thank you *JimmyLee*! You have helped me more than you will ever know.

To all the schools, community centers, church programs, individual parents and young CEO's – I appreciate, you believing in our program, your understanding and your patience. May plenty of blessings come your way.

JEWEL L DOMINO GROUP LLC / ©2015
5 Lawrence Street, Unit 328, Bloomfield, NJ 07003
(201) 259-6446 | jeweldominof@gmail.com | www.vondorinstitute.org

TABLE OF CONTENTS

SECTION 1

Who are you?	1
Education & Careers	3
Assets	7
Liabilities	9
debt & credit	11
investments	13
Bonus – black wall street	15

SECTION 2

entrepreneurship	19
the young ceo business plan	21

APPENDIX

Progress Notes
start-up expenses work sheets
About the author

Section I

Who are you?

It is very important to know who you are. One way to figure this out is to learn about where you come from. Knowing your family history and your back ground is the most logical approach to this fascinating journey.

Learning about your mothers' and fathers' heritage can open your eyes to a whole new world of possibilities and can answer a lot of questions you may have always had. You may have wondered, why is it that your mother always fixes things around the house when you break something or why is it that your father is always asked to sing and play the piano at all the family functions? The easiest way to find out the answers to these questions is to "ASK". Talk to your parents, grandparents, aunts, uncles, great cousins, etc.

When some or (if you are lucky) most of your questions are answered, you can then begin to learn about your own habits or talents. You can concentrate on what is your best skill or what it is you would like to work on. Now you have an idea of who can help put you on the right track to mastering your craft or what it is you have a passion for.

Now it is time you start feeding that very big, intelligent brain of yours by going home and interviewing your parents or paying a visit to grandpa or Aunt Brenda and getting the answers to the questions on the next page. Let them know that this is the greatest opportunity they will ever apply for, the position of being your "*MENTOR*".

What do you want to do?
_____
_____
_____
_____
_____
_____
_____
_____

What will make you happy?
_____
_____
_____
_____
_____
_____
_____
_____

What are you willing to do every day, all day in order to get what you want?
_____
_____
_____
_____
_____
_____
_____
_____

Where do your family come from?
_____
_____
_____
_____
_____
_____
_____
_____

{This last question is a very important question. It's good to know where you come from so that you can work on where you would like to go in life. Knowing your families' history is very important and can be very fulfilling. You learn what your past relatives did and how they survived. It can be a sense of pride!

Education

EDUCATION IS EXTREMELY IMPORTANT!

- **High School Diploma** – most important of all because here is where you learn the basics of what you need to get through life

- **Trade School** – is good for careers in where you will concentrate in a specialized area, ex., auto mechanic, HVAC, billing specialist

- **Professional Certification** – compliments the career choice you are already in or it can be very beneficial if you want to change careers

COLLEGE – NEEDED AND WANTED FOR A WHOLE VARIETY OF DIFFERENT REASONS

- Go if this is what **YOU** want
- Gain knowledge for yourself and not because you think it will get you a good safe J.O.B.
- Study PSAT's, SAT's, LSAT's, ACT's, etc.
- Be well rounded
- Get great written recommendations from 4 to 5 of your favorite teachers, your minister, the neighbor you baby sit for, etc.
- Do community service, volunteer, work in the summer or get part-time J.O.B.
- Join a club or 2, play a sport or 2
- Take a foreign language for a minimum of 2 years

FINANCIAL EDUCATION

- Learn all that you can about investing and saving
- Very important if your goal is to become *"financially self-sufficient"*

food for thought
Public school support is based on the taxes that community pays
{not fair and not right}

BEST WAY TO LEARN IS BY DOING!

You can only blame you for what you do with your money, not the system

- Not the government's fault
- No longer your mother's fault
- No longer your father's fault

CAREERS

A good education is most helpful when it comes to landing the ideal career. Employers would rather have an employee that has been educated beyond high school. Some college or a certificate is more appealing to a future employer than only holding a GED or high school diploma.

JOBS

Having a job can definitely pay the bills but will you be happy with a position that goes nowhere for the next 5 to 10 years? Some jobs have a cap on what you can make per hour no matter how long you have been with the company. Will you be happy with that?

{Keep in mind, a lot of JOB's, now days, require that you have at least a high school diploma - if not, at least a GED is needed in order to even fill out an application.}

Question?

What is a GED?
_____

What is the difference between a GED and a high school diploma?
_____

_____

If you want to go to college, name three universities or colleges that you would like to apply to.
_____

_____

_____

If you want to take up a trade, name two trade schools you would like to apply to.
_____

_____

List two different types of certifications that can be earned with or without a college degree.
_____

_____

What is the difference between a *job* and a *career*?
_____

_____

ASSETS

Make money while you sleep!

What is an *asset*?

(noun) - items of ownership convertible into cash; total resources of a person or business, as cash, notes and accounts receivable, securities, inventories, goodwill, fixtures, machinery, or real estate (opposed to liabilities).

Investments are assets – ex. stocks, bonds, commodities, land, *{house?}*

"Dang. I was hoping for oil."

Question?

Name four assets of any kind.

_____

_____

Name one way to acquire an asset.

_____

Name one way you can get money from an asset.

_____

What are stocks?

_____

_____

What are account receivables?

_____

_____

LIABILITIES

Going broke

Liability (noun) - moneys owed; debts or pecuniary obligations (opposed to assets).

These items will keep you working for the rest of your life. They take money out of your pocket!

Luxury items:
Your personal car, cell phone, your personal dwelling, expensive life style, etc.

Question?

How does something become a liability?

_____

_____

How can you get rid of a liability?

_____

_____

Name two liabilities that can be a necessity.

_____

Name two liabilities that are not needs.

_____

Name one liability that you just can't live without.

_____

DEBT & CREDIT

Debt can be good and bad / Learn about your credit and score!

GOOD DEBT:

Educational loans – this is considered good debt because you are trying to better your situation in life by furthering your education.

Mortgage on rental property – your tenants will pay rent which in turns pays off the mortgage. If you handle your finances correctly, this will also put some money in your pocket and you can possibly live rent free.

Leasing a vehicle for your business – helps you to make money for your business and is a nice tax write off on your business taxes.

BAD DEBT:

Credit card debt (if abused)
Charge card debt (if abused)
Personal car loan
Personal mortgage loan

Your **Credit history** can start to develop as soon as you turn 18 years of age (or possibly earlier). Start out small and slow. Maybe one credit card with a low limit and pay your bill in full, on time, every month!
If you cannot pay it in full within 3 months & on time every month, don't use it!

A **Credit score** is the number that is created to measure how well you do with payments to your creditors. The higher your credit score, the better. A credit score can be as high as an 850 and as low as a 450, 650 is about average.
- The higher your credit score the lower your interest rate in most cases.
- The lower your credit score the higher your interest rate in most cases.

All kinds of companies use your credit score to determine what they will charge you including but not limited to *car insurance companies*. Some companies go by your credit score to determine if they will hire you or not, for example, *banks*.

Question?

What kind of good debt would you mind not having?

_____

_____

What kind of bad debt would you try to stay away from?

_____

_____

Have you or anyone you know ever ordered their credit report / score or both?

_____

_____

If you had a chance to get a credit card, would you?

_____

_____

What would you want your credit score to be?

_____

_____

INVESTMENTS

For your present & future

Investment – (noun) An asset or item that is purchased with the hope that it will generate income or appreciate in the future.

In an economic sense, an investment is the purchase of goods that are not consumed today but are used in the future to create wealth.

In finance, an investment is a monetary asset purchased with the idea that the asset will provide income in the future or appreciate and be sold at a higher price.

Example: computer software company, pizzeria restaurant, coca cola stock, apartment or office building

Question?

What is a short term investment?

_____

_____

What is a long term investment?

_____

_____

Is there such a thing as a bad investment?

_____

_____

Give one example of an investment that can appreciate.

_____

Name two investments you would like to have.

_____

_____

A Little Known Black History Fact

BLACK WALL STREET

Tulsa Oklahoma 1921 {also known as "Little Africa"}

June 1 1921 – bombed from the air by the "KKK" (Ku Klux Klan) and other city officials. In 12 hours little Africa burned to the ground.

1500 to 3000 blacks died
Up to 600 successful businesses lost – amongst them were:

21 churches, 21 restaurants, 30 grocery stores, 2 movie theaters, a hospital, a bank, a post office, libraries, schools, law offices, 6 airplanes, (privately owned) and a bus system

Little Africa was compared to a mini Beverly Hills.

"The black dollar circulated 36 to 100 times; sometimes taking up to a year before it left the black community."

{Today, the black dollar leaves our black community in less than 15 minutes to make other communities rich.}

Dr. Berry owned the bus system. On a good day he brought in about $500 in earnings which was a lot in 1910.

A lot of black doctors owned their own medical school.

There were pawn shops, brothels and jewelry stores everywhere.

The entire state of Oklahoma had only 2 airports and yet 6 of the airplanes between the 2 airports where owned by blacks.

The 600 businesses consist of 36 square blocks with a population of 15,000 blacks.

The average black child that was a product of "black wall street" went to school in a suit and tie.

"NEPOTISM" was the one word they truly believed in.
- (a noun) patronage bestowed or favoritism shown on the basis of family relationship, as in business or politics

The main street in little Africa was "Greenwood Avenue" which was intersected by "Archer Street and Pine Street". This is how the famous "GAP Band" came up with their name, for they were from Tulsa Oklahoma and were very proud of the legend of "Black Wall Street".

Oklahoma was set aside to be a Black and Indian state

- There were 28 black townships
- 1/3 were blacks who traveled alongside the Indians which was known as the terrifying "Trail of Tears" between 1830 and 1842
- The people chose a black governor who was a treasurer in Kansas City
The treasurer (McDade) was threaten by the KKK that if he took office, they would kill him in 48hrs
- A lot of blacks owned farmland
- Many blacks went into the oil business
- Blacks depended upon each other because of the "Jim Crow Laws"

If someone's home burned down, it would be rebuilt by neighbors within a couple of weeks.

When blacks married Indians, some received their promised 40 acres and a mule and any oil that was later found on the land.

Black Wall Street conducted a lot of global business.

The victims of this horrid deed were never given restitution for this wrong; Insurance proceeds were never paid to survivors or to the families of the deceased.

1. Information is courtesy of Davey D's Hip Hop Corner
2. Other facts researched from other reputable internet source

Section II

ENTREPRENEUR

Communities & Entrepreneurship

What is an *entrepreneur*?
(noun/ French), plural - **entrepreneurs**

1. a person who organizes and manages any enterprise, especially a business, usually with considerable initiative and risk.

2. an employer of productive labor; contractor.

ENTREPRENEUR (CONT.)

An *entrepreneur* see's a problem and tries to find a solution, all the while profiting from his or her idea.

They figure out a way to put people to work once the idea is implemented hence helping that community to prosper by bringing in revenue.

Revenue be gets income; income is spent with in that community; taxes are paid by both residents and business owners of that community.

Taxes pay for better schools, policing, health care, etc., thus helping to put that community on the path to self-sustainability, responsibility, and PRIDE.

THE YOUNG CEO BUSINESS PLAN

1 Give Your Business a Name

Pick a name or logo you like that can be easy to recognize. Try to make it one of a kind. You cannot register your name or logo if it is like someone or something that is already registered.

Your Name and or Logo:

2 Legal Business Entity

Sole Proprietor – if it's only you, you will use your social security number; your 100% responsible for everything; you can be sued for everything; fewer taxes; free to start up; you keep 100% of both profits and losses.

General Partnership – same as above but includes two or more people (usually not married couples) and normally includes a written agreement.

Limited Partnership – cost to register; needs tax ID number; is composed of one or more general partners and one or more limited partners. The general partners manage the business and share fully in its profits and losses. Limited partners share in the profits of the business, but their losses are limited to the extent of their investment. Limited partners are usually not involved in the day-to-day operations of the business.

Limited Liability Partnership (LLP) – cost to register; needs tax ID number; is similar to a General Partnership except that normally a partner doesn't have personal liability for the negligence of another partner. This business structure is used most by professionals, such as accountants and lawyers.

Limited Liability Company (LLC) – You or you plus others own the company; cost to register; needs tax ID number; your liability is limited in that the business is sued in most cases; you or you plus others keep all profits

S (sub) – Corporation – (mainly for smaller corporations) need board of directors; same as above but can pay same taxes as LLC; can only sell up to 100 shares to others

Corporation – (mainly for big corporations) very expensive to start; double taxed; can get some tax breaks that other structures cannot: need board of directors; no limit on number of shares sold to the public; liability falls on corporation in most situations.

Benefit Corporation {new} – only a few states have adopted this structure and NJ being one of them; same as above but pays taxes on some income, not all; formed as a social benefit to the masses in some form or another.

Your Entity:

3   Describe Your Business

What will you offer?

Where will your business be (location)?

What are your hours of operation?

What will your business look like?

Who's on your management team?

Who will supply you with what you need for your business?

Who's on your financial team? {Accountant, Bookkeeper, Payroll, Banker}

Who's on your legal team?

4   Marketing Your Business

{This part of your plan is very important! This is how you will make your MONEY!}

Who will you sell your product or service to? {Who needs it or want it?}

Is your business seasonal?

How much will it cost to make your product? How much will you sell it for or how much will you charge for your service?

How will you market your product or service?

Who's your competition?

5   Proof that you will make a great entrepreneur/ business owner

In order to back up the statements you may have made in your business plan, you may need to include any or all of the following documents in your appendix:

- *Personal resumes*
- *Personal financial statements*
- *Credit reports, business and personal*
- *Copies of leases*
- *Letter of reference*
- *Contracts*
- *Legal documents*
- *Personal and business tax returns*
- *Miscellaneous relevant documents.*
- *Photographs*

Benefits of Entrepreneurship

Sky's the limit!!!

Make as much money as you want! It's your business! No one can tell you how much you are worth or how many hours you *must* work or cannot work, that is all up to you.

You set your hours, days, weeks, months, years. Go in when you want, stay as late as you want, leave as early as you want, take lunch when you want and as long as you want. No one can tell you when, where or how long to be, that is totally up to you.

Best of all - vacation when you want!

BEWARE!

Things like paying taxes, insurances, licenses, etc., all come with making money, owning a business, being an investor. These things can sneak up on you and before you know it, the money is gone. This is why having a very good accountant is very important but you will learn all of this as you grow and become successful.

Know that "*you*" are responsible for your paycheck and the paychecks of your employees. If you don't run your business right, you will go out of business.

Good luck!

And remember "NEPOTISM" (*a noun/ Italian*) is key.

Take care of your *family* and *community* and they will take care of you.

Date	Progress Notes

Answer Key

(Pg. 6) General Education Diploma; The first difference most people will notice is the difference in the age requirements. In most places, a person can take the GED at any time after they are 16 years old. For a high school diploma, a student may need to invest as much as four years, although many people manage to complete high school in as little as three years. A GED is a seven-hour test on five subject areas. If you want to go to a university or a four-year college, you may want to consider getting a high school diploma, or if that isn't possible, spend a year at a community college so you can demonstrate your academic skill to a college or a university; ex. Everest, Itt Tech; ex. Lincoln Tech, Educational Leadership.

(Pg. 8) ex. business machinery, cash, stock, apartment building; ex. inherit; ex. rent; stock – is a share in the ownership of a company; account receivables – money owed by customers to an entity (or individual) in exchange for goods or services that has been delivered or used, but not yet paid for.

(Pg. 10) ex. buy it on credit; ex. pays it off; ex. phone, car; ex. big fancy house, more than one personal car.

(Pg. 12) ex. educational loan; credit cards.

(Pg. 14) short term investment – stocks and bonds that can be liquidated fairly quickly; long term investment – stocks, bonds, real estate, cash, that will be held for a year or longer; ex. real estate.

STARTUP EXPENSES

BEGIN BY ESTIMATING EXPENSES
What will it cost you to get your business up and running? The key to accuracy here is attention to detail. For each category of expense, draw up a list of everything you will need to purchase. This will include both tangible assets (for example, equipment, inventory) and services (for example, remodeling, insurance). Then determine where you might purchase these goods or services. Research more than one vendor; i.e.: comparison shop. Do not look at price alone; terms of payment, delivery, reliability, and service are also important.

STARTUP EXPENSES

CAPITAL EQUIPMENT LIST	AMOUNT
Furniture	
Equipment	
Other	
Total	

LOCATION AND ADMIN EXPENSES	AMOUNT
Rental	
Utility deposits	
Legal and accounting fees	
Prepaid insurance	
Pre-opening salaries	
Other	
Total	

OPENING INVENTORY	AMOUNT
Category 1	
Category 2	
Category 3	
Category 4	
Total	

ADVERTISING AND PROMOTIONAL EXPENSES	AMOUNT
Advertising	
Signage	
Printing	
Travel/entertainment	
Other/additional categories	
Total	

OTHER EXPENSES	AMOUNT
Other expense 1	
Other expense 2	
Total	

Reserve for Contingencies

Working Capital

ADD A RESERVE FOR CONTINGENCIES
Be sure to explain in your narrative how you decided on the amount you are putting into this reserve.

DETERMINE YOUR CASH FLOW
You cannot open with an empty bank account. You need a cash cushion to meet expenses while the business gets going. Eventually you should do a 12-month cash flow projection.

ENTER YOUR SOURCES OF CAPITAL
Now that you have estimated how much capital will be needed to start, you should turn your attention to the top part of this worksheet. Enter the amounts you will put in yourself, how much will be injected by partners or investors, and how much will be supplied by borrowing.

SOURCES OF CAPITAL

OWNERS' INVESTMENT (NAME & OWNERSHIP %) — AMOUNT

- Your name and percent ownership
- Other investor
- Other investor
- Other investor
- **Total**

OTHER LOANS — AMOUNT

- Source 1
- Source 2
- **Total**

SUMMARY STATEMENT

SOURCE OF CAPITAL — TOTALS

- Owners' and other investments
- Other loans
- **Total**

STARTUP EXPENSES — TOTALS

- Capital equipment
- Location/administration expenses
- Opening inventory
- Advertising/promotional expenses
- Other expenses
- Working capital
- **Total**

SECURITY AND COLLATERAL FOR LOAN PROPOSAL

COLLATERAL FOR LOANS	DESCRIPTION	VALUE
Other collateral		
Other collateral		
Total		

OWNERS

Your name here

Other owner

Other owner

LOAN GUARANTORS (OTHER THAN OWNERS)

Loan guarantor 1

Loan guarantor 2

Loan guarantor 3

ABOUT THE AUTHOR

Jewel L. Domino

Born in Union, NJ, raised in Irvington, NJ, attended and graduated from the Irvington public school system. Attended NYIT for two years from 1992 thru 1994, and in 2000, graduated from NJIT with a Bachelor's of science in management.

While attending NJIT and after volunteering to make 2 dishes for NSBE, she started a small business catering which she picked up from her mother after being asked to cook a few dishes for NJIT, Rutgers and Essex County college clubs and organizations. While working full time as an administrative assistant and working part-time for a small promotions company to help pay her tuition, she ended up branching off from the promotions company to go into business for herself after noticing how much money she was clearing in commission alone.

After graduating from NJIT and at her father's request, she went to work for several major corporations but was never satisfied working for someone else. So after her grant funded position at NJIT in 2009 came to an end, she decided once again to go into business for herself.

After being told about a restaurant start-up opportunity by a family member, she rented a small kitchen in the iron bound section of Newark, NJ, which served both soul food and American home cooking, catering to small contracts with both big and small businesses and foot traffic from the locals that supported her strongly.

Entering into a bad professional agreement with the owners of the kitchen, caused her to shut down and go back to work a year later. After working for only two years, she had to have a major surgery which put her out of the heavy construction field for the rest of her life. Once again she decided to go into business for herself but this time with a yearning to teach youth entrepreneurship. This came about while working for NJIT and speaking with the youth and their parents. She realized that what she was doing was not fulfilling at all and wanted to tell the youth the "real deal" about higher education and entrepreneurship and she knew that while working for any institute of higher education, she would not be able to fill this yearning.

Over the years, different institutions, individuals and businesses continued to stay in touch with her and invite her to speak to their students or at their events or join their organizations. That's when she knew she had something. She had an "ear" or five that would listen to her, that believed in what she was trying to do and welcomed her with open arms to introduce her vision to their "Young CEO's".

Jewel has two wonderful children that she loves more than life itself, a huge loving family and a few unbelievable friends that are made of pure sugar {Leslie}.

"I thank everyone from the bottom of my heart for believing in what it is I am trying to do and for picking up this workbook however you have gotten your hands on it." – Jewel

Peace and Blessings in abundance!!!

www.ingramcontent.com/pod-product-compliance
Lightning Source LLC
Chambersburg PA
CBHW061358090426
42743CB00002B/64